THE ULTIMATE COURSE CREATION GUIDE
How to Grow Your Business with an Online Course in 8 Weeks or Less

©2022 Sophie Higgins

All Rights Reserved. Printed in the U.S.A.

ISBN: 978-1-947276-12-3
ASIN: B0BKQKTLMF

All rights reserved. No part of this book may be reproduced or transmitted in any form or by any means, electronic or mechanical, including photocopying, recording, or by an information storage and retrieval system - except by a reviewer who may quote brief passages in a review to be printed in a magazine or newspaper - without permission in writing from the author.

Publishing and Design:

EPIC AUTHOR
PUBLISHING

Ordering Information: Quantity sales. Special discounts are available on quantity purchases by corporations, associations, and others. Orders by U.S. trade bookstores and wholesalers. For details, contact the publisher below:

Contact: 561-601-9871 | info@epicauthor.com | EpicAuthor.com

First Edition

THE ULTIMATE COURSE CREATION GUIDE

How To **Grow Your Business** With An Online Course In 8 Weeks Or Less

SOPHIE H HIGGINS
FOREWORD BY DR. IVAN MISNER, FOUNDER OF BNI

THE FREE ULTIMATE COURSE CREATION GUIDE COMPANION COURSE

To help guide you through this book, I created a *free bonus companion course* that includes downloadable worksheets, bonus video content, and resources and links mentioned in this book. *This is the first step toward your success*, so I highly recommend you sign up now.

The supplemental materials in this *free course* are organized by the sections and chapters of this book, making it easy for you to find what you need as you read along.

In addition, I want you to know that *you are not alone*. We have a private course community of amazing people who are just like you. Please come hang out with your new tribe to find support and encouragement on your journey. You get access by going to the link below.

REVIEWS

"*Thank you, Sophie! I really appreciate all the hard work you've put into this course. It's a great value! All the resources are priceless. I now just have to put my head down and USE them!*"
—**Susan Alden, Co-Founder of Mind Body Aloha Wellness & Nrf2 Warrior**

"*I have had this idea of developing an online course to help entrepreneurs write their business plan for years. Until I met Sophie, it was always just an idea. Sophie Higgins helped me take that idea and created a storyboard that we then developed the course from. Not only is Sophie brilliant at developing meaningful curriculum, but she is also knowledgeable with technology that actually saved me money and made everything look professional. She took me step by step from developing the program, creating the platform, and even marketing and pricing of the course. I would have never been able to do this on my own. I am tremendously grateful for Sophie's expertise and dedication but most of all for her caring attitude.*"
—**Joann Seery, Owner, Serious Business Solutions, Inc.**

"*Sophie is a brilliant educator and course creator. I've had the opportunity to work with her and what she brings to the table is unlike any other resource I've seen. Her background in education is perfect for figuring out how to present deep learning that's engaging for the audience. What's the point of an online course if it's not interesting, right? More than just a place to film an online course, Sophie's ability to help craft the best possible version of the course is unmatched. I'm so glad I know Sophie.*"
—**Michael Liebowitz, Messaging and Value Articulation Specialist Leveraging Behavioral Neurology**

"I met Sophie on LinkedIn when I was looking for someone to write articles for one of my clients. After a brief Zoom call, I quickly realized Sophie was much more than a copywriter. I invited Sophie to share her approach to copywriting and article writing with my mastermind group. Sophie blew us away with her structured approach to article writing and copywriting. ***She's a fantastic teacher, and her methodology is simple, but very powerful.*** *A simple four-step process helps you create articles that people want to read. I highly recommend connecting with Sophie and hiring her to help with your copywriting and articles."*

—Ted Prodromou, Bestselling Author of Ultimate Guide to LinkedIn for Business

TABLE OF CONTENTS

Foreword xi
Message From The Author xv
    My journey..xvi
    The 4 Phases Of Building A Course xx
    Know The End Goal For Your Audience xxii
    Discovery Questionnaire................................... xxvi

WEEK 1: HOW TO FIND YOUR REALLY HELPFUL ONLINE EDUCATION TOPIC!..................... 1
    Your Unique Combination 3
    Your Audience Burning Desire Worksheet 4
    SMART-ER Goals Worksheet 6

WEEK 2: HOW TO WRITE AND TEST YOUR IRRESISTIBLE ONLINE COURSE OFFER 9
    Your Transformational Course
    Topic Headline Worksheet.................................. 10
    Your Market Research Worksheet 13
    Audience Research Survey 18

WEEK 3: SET A WINNING COMPETITION BASED PRICING STRATEGY FOR YOUR ONLINE COURSE 23
    Competitive Research Template 23
    Your Financial Model 26

WEEK 4: HOW TO DEVELOP YOUR EFFECTIVE TRANSFORMATIONAL COURSE OUTLINE................. 29
    Your Course Mind Map...................................... 31
    Your Course Outline Worksheet 33

WEEK 5: HOW TO CREATE A SIMPLE AND EFFECTIVE STORYBOARD FOR YOUR ONLINE COURSE 37
- What Is A Content Storyboard? 39
- Storyboard Example 42
- Your Content Storyboard 45

WEEK 6: EFFECTIVELY ORGANIZE YOUR ONLINE COURSE IN YOUR LEARNING MANAGEMENT PLATFORM 49
- Your Course Structure Guide 50
- Example Module Introduction 56
- Your Course Setup Checklist 57

WEEK 7: RIG YOUR ONLINE COURSE LAUNCH STRATEGY WITH EXCITING AND EFFECTIVE SALES COPY 59
- Copy For The Sales Page 60
- Launch Schedule Template 68
- Launch Schedule For Your Online Course— Email Campaign & Social Posts 69

WEEK 8: HOW TO EASILY PLAN, RUN, AND RECORD YOUR LIVE SESSIONS AND PREPARE FOR BETTER RELAUNCH 73
- Guide To Plan And Run Live Lessons 74
- Improve Your Course For The Relaunch 80
- Your Lesson Agenda Outline 81
- Lesson Plan Outline Template For A Webinar 82

WHAT'S NEXT? 87

FOREWORD

Foreword by Dr. Ivan Misner, Founder & Chief Visionary Officer of BNI (Business Network International)

As Founder and Chief Visionary Officer of Business Network International (BNI), the world's largest business networking organization, I see firsthand the importance of education in networking and when you are building and running a business. What I call the leaky bucket syndrome often happens when passing on information in large organizations and in general.

The leaky bucket syndrome happens when you teach me how to do something and some information leaks out. Then I teach someone else how to do that, and a little more information leaks. Then my student teaches a third or fourth person how to do something, and now more information leaks.

What happens is that you now have half a bucket of information. And when you have half a bucket of information, people look at it, saying: "That doesn't look right. That is wrong." And what do they do? They start putting their own stuff in. People are probably going to put their own things in any way, and you have to be careful about that. That's called feature creep. But feature creep is on steroids when you have leaky bucket syndrome.

To minimize the harmful effects of the leaky bucket syndrome and feature creeping, I realized in 1986 that we had to have manuals when we did the BNI training. And the manuals had to be in writing, and everybody had to work off the same manuals. People still get off the trail, and sometimes we must bring them back. But I think the key is to help people avoid leaky bucket syndrome.

Like Sophie, education is my passion. The BNI Foundation supports children in education. Children represent 20 percent of the world's population, but they are 100 percent of our future. To me, education is crucial, and it goes along with one of my favorite expressions:

"You may not be able to make a world of difference, but you can make a difference in the world."

Sophie and I share the emphasis on edutainment and applying what you learn. **Theory is no good if you can't apply it!** You need to entertain people while teaching them. If you lecture, people will go to sleep. You need to tell stories, and you need to bring the knowledge to life. Get them to DO the exercises so that they get engaged in learning.

In *The Ultimate Course Creation Guide*, Sophie shows you how to develop a robust educational program in bite-size pieces. She helps you clarify WHO your audience is, WHAT challenges they have, and HOW you can help them transform their lives and get the desired outcome. When you look at your online program through the eyes of your audience, it is much easier to include WHAT they need to know and WHY, and then show them HOW to apply what they are learning.

Sophie's approach to course creation reminds me of a recent conversation with Richard Branson, founder of the Virgin Group.

He said, "Any fool can make something complex. It's the really smart person who simplifies it."

What I admire most about Sophie and her approach to growing your business with online courses is that she is a very experienced educator. Her practical experience shows in all her templates and guides throughout the book. Sophie wants you to be successful and build the business and life of your dreams. For example, she encourages you to see your online course as one of the tiers in the financial model for your business. If your audience wants more personalized help, you can offer your coaching and consulting services in addition to your online courses. I also like the way she recommends you repurpose your course content into books and articles to grow your visibility and build your credibility, which, when done with consistency, will lead to your profitability.

I see that the future of face-to-face communication is online. The technology is advancing at such a rate into mixed reality, Metaverse, and 3D technology, that the future will be online. And because the future will be online, **I highly recommend Sophie's book and course creation support services if you want to embrace the future and grow your business with edutaining programs online.**

Ivan Misner, Ph.D.
Founder of BNI
New York Times Bestselling Author

MESSAGE FROM THE AUTHOR

What if you can grow your business by sharing your passion with the world? And what if you can help more people without working long hours and make money while you sleep?

Sounds great, right?

You can do it!

This book is the ultimate guide to help you grow your business with an online course in 8 weeks or less. I designed the book to take you through the process of creating your online course week by week to make sure you cover all the basics, from idea clarification to content development to choosing a learning management system (LMS) to host your course content and getting ready for your first test launch. The course will also teach you to create a customer experience funnel for future relaunches.

Maybe you haven't thought about how having an online course as part of your coaching or consulting business can be a valuable source of income. **With an evergreen on-demand course, you add a passive income stream to your business**. In addition, having an online program as part of your business will add to your reputation as an expert and authority and create a source of content you can repurpose into books, presentations, and other resources.

Maybe you already know that having an online course as part of your coaching or consulting business is a great idea, but you don't know how to get it done without spending hours and hours gathering your thoughts. Or maybe you just don't know where to start.

You might know you could be helping more people and work smarter, not harder, by duplicating yourself with an online course. You are also aware that **an online program will reinforce your brand identity as a qualified expert and add to your library of intellectual property.** Furthermore, you might know you are leaving money on the table by not taking advantage of the passive income you can generate from having an online course as part of your business.

In other words, an online program is a great way to share your unique wisdom with the world and grow passive income for your business at the same time. You have the opportunity to duplicate yourself like a good version of Mr. Smith from *The Matrix*. Instead of repeating the same things over and over. You might as well put some of that information into an on-demand program. You can always upsell with group sessions or individual sessions where your client can receive more personalized access to your valuable time and insights.

That is working smarter, not harder!

My Journey

I help experts like you create meaningful and profitable online courses by transforming their unique wisdom into a well-crafted empowering learning experience.

In January 2019, I chose to follow my heart and dream of an entrepreneurial lifestyle. I left everything I had in Denmark and headed to America with my new American husband and anything I could fit in one big suitcase.

Starting all over in my new country has been both exciting and challenging. Building a new business from scratch. Getting to use my twenty-plus years of experience in the learning industry in

Denmark to help coaches and consultants grow their businesses with meaningful and profitable online programs globally.

My Online Course Creation Support Services **helps experts share their unique talents, passion, and expertise and reach more people.** I help my clients consolidate their position as experts in their field and duplicate themselves to free up time and generate revenue while they sleep at the same time.

I am excited to use my unique background as a learning expert, well-known speaker, educational consultant, author of six textbooks, and high school principal to help my clients reach their goals. **I LOVE learning!** To me, learning is the pathway to freedom.

And I want to help you **grow** your business with online courses.

Please let me welcome you to this ultimate guide to help you create your online course.

I created this ultimate course creation guide after several requests from my students who said, "Sophie, please put all these valuable templates and guidelines into a book so we can use them more than once to create more classes."

With that, I have created a **FREE** companion course to use with this book.

https://courses.sophiehhiggins.com/courses/the-ultimate-course-creation-guide-how-to-grow-your-business-with-an-online-course?coupon=freewithultimatebook

And if you want a more in-depth explanation of how to take each step, you are welcome to join my flagship course that explains each of the steps in this book in detail. If you follow the link below, you get 50 percent off the regular course price.

MESSAGE FROM THE AUTHOR

https://courses.sophiehhiggins.com/courses/Create-Meaningful-Online-Courses-And-Grow-Passive-Income?coupon=ultimateguide

All the steps, tools, and templates have been developed, tested, and refined after working with many clients and helping them build their meaningful and profitable programs.

Here is what some of my clients have said after working through the steps of the course creation process with me.

"It has been an amazing experience working with Sophie for my leadership course "Mastering the Business Basics" Sophie's expertise and system for course creation have proven to work well for busy senior business advisors and coaches like me. I am proud of completing my course, which will make an impact on women entrepreneurs' journeys."

—Roz Huang, Founder/CEO, Dandelion Global,
Global Business Development & Co-Founder/CEO,
Athena Music & Wellness Therapy

"When I was considering hiring a course development course, the first thing I wanted was a depth of experience combined with a passion for people and learning, and I found all of that and more in Sophie! Not only does she help you with the content, course development, and the overall mechanics of creating an online course, she gives invaluable feedback from the lens of the "student" taking the course. I was able to refine and enhance my content in a way that will help the student through the desired transformation, which is the ultimate outcome of success for the student.

Beyond her depth of experience in education, business, and learning & development, Sophie is a wonderful human and was so much fun to work with because she brings her expertise and passion to the calls! Sophie cares about her clients and her work, and it shows in her ability to help people create courses that bring value to the learner.

I highly recommend Sophie to anyone looking to design and launch a personal or professional transformation course! She is AMAZING!"
 —Faith Geiger, LMSW, Executive Coach to Conscious Leaders | Workplace Mental Health & Psychedelic-Assisted Therapist in Training | Workplace Culture & Employee Experience Consultant

"I have had this idea of developing an online course to help entrepreneurs write their business plan for years. Until I met Sophie, it was always just an idea. Sophie Higgins helped me take that idea and created a storyboard that we then developed the course from. Not only is Sophie brilliant at developing meaningful curriculum, she is knowledgeable with technology that actually saved me money and made everything look professional. She took me step by step from developing the program, creating the platform, and even marketing and pricing of the course. **I would have never been able to do this on my own**. *I am tremendously grateful for Sophie's expertise and dedication but most of all for her caring attitude."*
 —Joann Seery, Owner, Serious Business Solutions, Inc.

I'm genuinely excited to welcome you to this ultimate guide that is designed to take you through the four phases you need to create a meaningful and profitable online course, reach new clients and expand your business offerings with additional programs to grow your business.

I believe everyone has something **unique** to share with the world, and I'm on a mission to help 1,000+ people quit their day jobs by helping them create an **online course** and **make money** on something they are passionate about. That is why I have written *The Ultimate Course Creation Guide* for you.

Let's dive in!

MESSAGE FROM THE AUTHOR

4 PHASES TO CREATE YOUR SUCCESSFUL ONLINE COURSE

4 phases you should do to create a meaningful and profitable video course

STEP 1. IDEA CLARIFICATION
The first phase is all about discovering your audience's problems and how you can provide a unique solution.

STEP 2. CONTENT CREATION
When the end goal is clear it is much easier to create the content your audience needs to get the outcome they desire.

STEP 3. LMS PRODUCTION
In this phase, you set up your course in LMS. Record your videos and presentations. Consider live sessions to test and get feedback.

STEP 4. LAUNCH & RELAUNCH
Test and upload your videos to your LMS. And create your customer experience funnel for successful launch and relauch.

REMINDER
- You are unique and have a lot to offer!
- You can duplicate yourself, help more people simultaniously, and make money while you sleep.

NEED HELP?
Check out our course creation support services:
https://sophiehhiggins.com

The infographic shows you the four phases I am going to take you through during the course creation process, step by step, to help you grow your business with an online course. The steps are based on best practices established during years of creating courses and helping other people build their courses.

One of the most important things when creating a course is to know the end goal and the steps to get there. Because **when you know where you're heading, you can reverse engineer the experience to help people to reach the desired goal.**

If you don't know what the end goal is and you just start teaching what comes to mind, it will end up being a confusing experience for your audience. And we don't want to confuse people, right?

Let me use the course example below to illustrate what the steps toward the end goal in a course transformation process can look like.

MESSAGE FROM THE AUTHOR

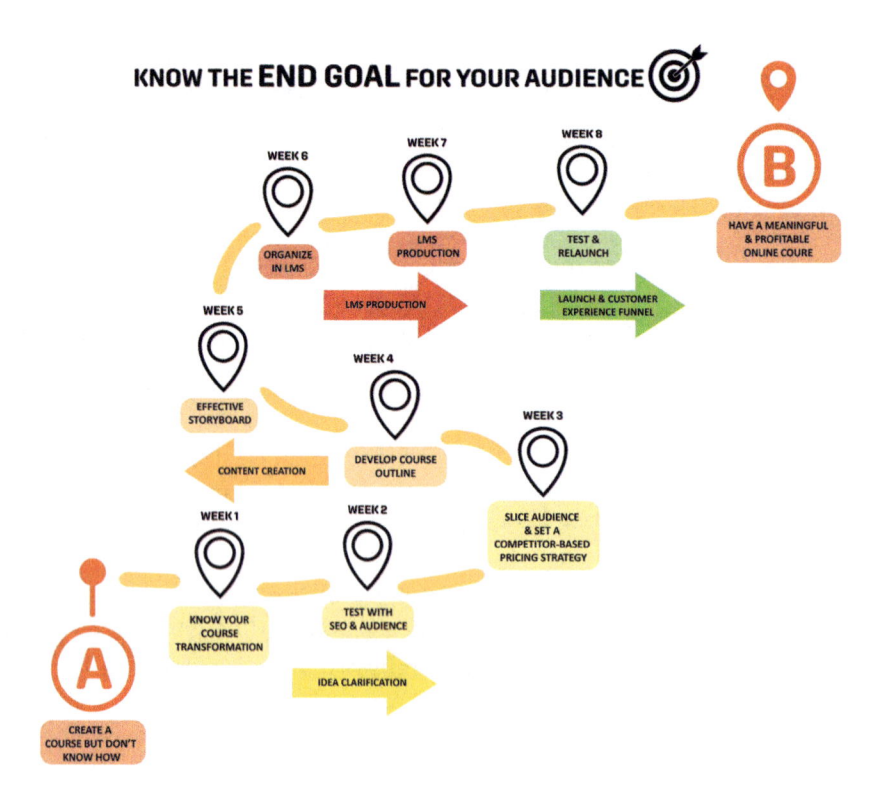

KNOW THE END GOAL FOR YOUR AUDIENCE

- **A** — CREATE A COURSE BUT DON'T KNOW HOW
- **WEEK 1** — KNOW YOUR COURSE TRANSFORMATION — IDEA CLARIFICATION
- **WEEK 2** — TEST WITH SEO & AUDIENCE
- **WEEK 3** — SLICE AUDIENCE & SET A COMPETITOR-BASED PRICING STRATEGY
- **WEEK 4** — DEVELOP COURSE OUTLINE
- **WEEK 5** — EFFECTIVE STORYBOARD — CONTENT CREATION
- **WEEK 6** — ORGANIZE IN LMS
- **WEEK 7** — LMS PRODUCTION
- **WEEK 8** — TEST & RELAUNCH — LAUNCH & CUSTOMER EXPERIENCE FUNNEL
- **B** — HAVE A MEANINGFUL & PROFITABLE ONLINE COURSE

In the above example, the end goal for my audience is to have a meaningful and profitable online course. That is point B for my audience. So that's what we're aiming for throughout the course and this book.

The current reality is the starting point A for my audience—you. **You know you want to create a course, but you might not know exactly how to go about creating it.** The transformation in the course and in this book is to take you from your current reality of wanting to create a course (point A) to your desired future (point B), which is the end goal of the course.

Between the starting point, point A, and the end goal, point B, is the transformation process. **The transformation process is designed to take you step by step in bite-size increments to reach the end goal.** The reason for this incremental process is that you cannot jump to the end goal in one jump, because if you could, *you would*.

The course transformation fills in the gaps of knowledge and how to implement new knowledge in bite-size pieces.

The first phase of the course creation process is the **idea clarification** phase. The idea clarification phase helps you define your unique course transformation based on your unique combination of talents, background, and experience. In this phase, you also learn how to write and test your irresistible course offer and test it for a SEO score and get audience feedback. SEO stands for Search Engine Optimization. The SEO score reflects how popular a topic is and how much this topic appears in average monthly searches.

The last part of the idea clarification phase is to slice the audience and set a competitor-based pricing strategy. The idea clarification phase is the foundational phase for the rest of the work in building a program for your business. It is like starting with the foundation when you build a house. Not having a solid foundation is like building a house directly on the sand. It doesn't last.

The second phase of the course creation process is the **content creation** phase. In this phase, you will develop the actual course outline, and you will be writing keywords for an effective storyboard to help you be cohesive and to the point when it is time for you to record your course.

The third phase will help you **organize and produce your course** and set your course up in a learning management system. Part of this phase is to get your course ready for the first launch and get the course ready to sell. In this phase, you get the templates and swipe files you need to write effective sales copy for your sales page.

The last phase of the course creation process is the **launch and relaunch** phase. In this phase, you get help to guide people through the customer experience funnel to turn your leads into customers with an email campaign and free webinar as a lead magnet. The idea is to test your course content and improve for future relaunches based on what you learn as an instructor through your first launch.

The point of testing your course is to think of course creation as a learning process. Every learning process is a cyclical process where you continually learn and improve your offer. My emphasis on testing is where my approach differs from some of the other course creators out there.

One of the big benefits of testing your course is, first of all, that you can make sure you have a good customer-market fit. You get a chance to actually test your offer and get feedback throughout the process. The biggest benefit of launching with a presale campaign is that you can make sure that you have an audience before you spend a lot of time developing video content.

The approach of testing with a live launch also gives you the opportunity to record and edit your course for your evergreen product while you are doing your live sessions. In other words, testing your course with a small audience is a smart way to create content for your evergreen course.

This ultimate course creation guide will lead you through the four phases of creating a meaningful and profitable online course. I structured the course and book as an eight-week program, but you can spend more or less time going through the process if you prefer.

THE ULTIMATE COURSE CREATION GUIDE

Before you start with course chapters, here are some steps you can take **right now** to prepare and get more clarity about the course creation process and your course idea.

Tasks To Get Started:

1. Watch the FREE webinar replay of the *4 Phases You Should Do To Create A Meaningful Online Course That Will Sell*

https://courses.sophiehiggins.com/courses/4-phases-you-should-do-to-create-a-meaningful-online-course-that-will-sell

2. Answer the questions in the discovery questionnaire below to start getting more clarity about your online course idea.

3. Start listening to your target audience on social media. What are they saying about their problems and the solutions they are seeking? And how is it that you can help them achieve their desired transformation?

Discovery Questionnaire

Before you start creating your course, I suggest you answer the questions below regarding your course idea. Your answers will help clarify your course structure and the value your course will provide for your audience and your business.

Target Audience
1. Who is your target audience?
2. What are they trying to achieve?
3. What are your target audience's common fears, frustrations, and problems?
4. What are their wants, needs, and desires?

Course Value
5. How is your course THE solution to their problems? What makes your approach different from the competitors?
6. What will your students be able to do that they were unable to do before they embarked on your course journey? What is the big end goal of your course?

Course Journey
7. What steps will they need to take with your guidance during the course to reach the big end goal — (what do they need to learn step by step, what are the pieces of the scaffold)?
8. How will they know they are moving in the right direction on their learning journey? What does success look like to the student?
9. What tasks and exercises can you include to help them consolidate the learning points?
10. Other ideas and things I need to know about your course?

Business Outcome
11. What will having this course do for your business?
12. What will you be able to do that you could not do before?

Week 1: How To Find Your Really Helpful Online Education Topic!

Helping people transform their lives is essential for having a meaningful and profitable online **course**.

Take a moment to think about the last course you bought . . .

- What moved you to buy that particular course?
- Why did you pick that course over other courses?

When we think about why we buy a course, we will likely find that we all have one major thing in common.

We are looking to get from **our current reality**, **Point A**, to our **desired future**, **Point B,** as easily and fast as possible. If we already knew how to get to Point B on our own, we wouldn't be buying a course. The journey that helps us get from our current reality to our desired future can be defined as **the course transformation**.

Lifelong learning and growth are primary human drives, along with our need for safety and belonging. Because of these fundamental human drivers, we need to ensure that our course fills a gap and brings our audience from point A to point B safely and meaningfully.

In other words, for your online course to be **profitable**, it must be **meaningful** to your audience.

Before buying a course, we want to ensure our guide is qualified and capable of helping us reach our goals safely and effectively. That is why we often look at reviews before we buy a course.

As course creators, we want to ensure that people know they can trust us. We want our audience to know that we are **the right guide** for them, and that we can help them get their desired transformation easier and better than if they went to someone else.

One way to build trust and belonging is to show our audience that we are "**LIKE-KIND**." Show people that we are just like them. For people who want to follow us, they will want to know that we have successfully overcome the same obstacles that they are currently facing and that we have found a way to reach the goal they are now seeking to reach. People will want to learn from us when they know that we have walked a similar path and gotten successfully from Point A to Point B.

Once your audience **KNOW**, **LIKE**, and **TRUSTS** you, they will want to hear how you can help them get the desired outcome.

In this chapter, you will get to know:

- What unique combination of skills, talents, background, and experience makes you the perfect transformational guide for your audience?
- What burning desire can you help your audience achieve based on your unique background and experience?
- What will your audience be able to do differently after taking your course? (Your course transformation)
- How do you invite your audience to relate to you as a trustworthy guide? Where do they find you?

The following exercises will help you answer these critical questions.

Your Unique Combination

This exercise will help you identify your sweet spot. Your sweet spot is your distinctive combination of skills, talents, passion, background, and experience that makes you unique and different from other course creators. Start by filling in keywords about **your special abilities and skills, talents and passion, and background and experience**. Do you see a unique combination that can be used to guide a course transformation that your audience desires?

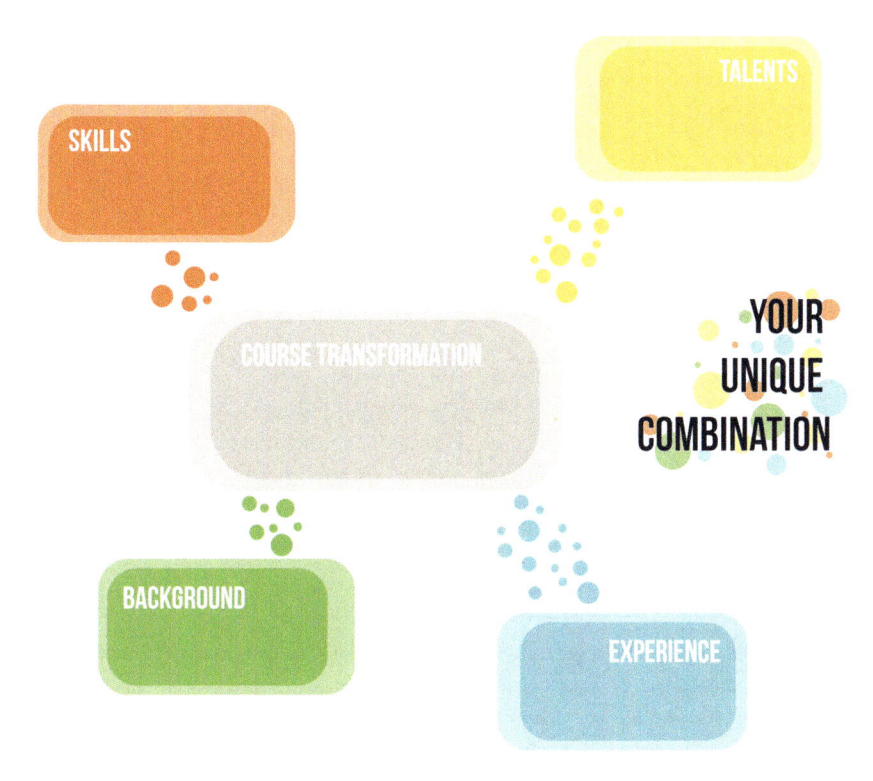

SKILLS

TALENTS

COURSE TRANSFORMATION

YOUR UNIQUE COMBINATION

BACKGROUND

EXPERIENCE

Now you have at least one idea about a course transformation you can help your audience achieve. You may have more than one idea. That's great! This means that you can create a series of courses.

The audience, competitor, and market research you will do later on will help you determine where to start and what course you want to create first.

Your Audience Burning Desire Worksheet

The audience burning desire worksheet will help you clarify what you know about your audience already. It will also help you think about what you would like to find out. These considerations will be helpful once you decide what questions you would like to ask your audience in your audience research.

What do you know about your audience?

- What is their burning desire?
- How do you KNOW?
- What do you THINK you know?
- What would you like to FIND OUT?

What will your audience be able to do differently after taking your course? ✏️
_____
_____

How will you help them get from their current Point A to their desired Point B? ✏️
_____
_____

Your course transformation notes ✏️
_____
_____

The main question for your course transformation is what your audience will be able to do differently after taking your course.

Some examples of course transformations for inspiration are:

- By the end of this course, I will know how to create a meaningful and profitable online course.
- By the end of this course, I will have written a business plan to present to the bank to get a loan to start my business.
- By the end of this course, I will know how people react to change in an organization and why, so I can lead the change process better as a manager.

You can continue the list of examples yourself.

By the end of this course, I will know how to . . .

Specific is better when you write your course transformation. It is easier to reach a clearly defined goal than to obtain a vague outcome. An example of an unclear course transformation could be:

- By the end of this course, I will be happy.
- By the end of this course, I will have a successful business.

These two examples of course transformations are too broad and ambiguous.

The SMART-ER Goals Worksheet will help you test if your course transformation is SMART-ER. The SMART-ER a headline, the more specific it is and the easier it is to understand what you are aiming to achieve.

SMART-ER Goals Worksheet

You can use the SMART-ER Goals worksheet to adjust your course transformation. Test if you need to make your transformation more **specific, measurable, attainable, relevant, and timebound**. In addition, you can consider how to **evaluate and reevaluate** if and how your students will reach the desired outcome of the course transformation. If some areas are vague, you can make adjustments.

The goal of the SMART-ER worksheet is to help you test if your course transformation is specific enough and if people can actually reach the end goal in a manner where they can track and evaluate their progress.

An example of a SMART-ER course transformation compared to the ambiguous statements above could be:

- By the end of this 7-month course, I will know what steps to take to be an active participant and feel more grounded and grateful in my life.

- By the end of this 8-week course, I will have written a business plan to help me lay the foundation for a successful business and secure the funding I need to get started.

THE ULTIMATE COURSE CREATION GUIDE

SMART-ER GOALS

Test if your course transformation is SMART-ER:

S PECIFIC

M EASUREABLE

A TTAINABLE

R ELEVANT

T IME

E VALUATE

R E-EVALUATE

Week 2: How To Write And Test Your Irresistible Online Course Offer

At this point, you have an idea of **the desired transformation** your course provides to your audience.

You also know how and why you are the unique guide to help them get from their current reality, Point A, to their desired future, Point B.

This week you will learn how to **write your irresistible online course offer** and **test** it.

By the end of this chapter, you will know:

- How to write your *hot* transformational course topic headline
- How to test your course headline and make sure your topic is something many people are searching for
- How to do market research
- How to do audience research to test your assumptions about your audience and the outcome they desire
- How to analyze the findings from your market and audience research and look for patterns

The next exercise is designed to help you write your irresistible course offer.

Your Transformational Course Topic Headline Worksheet

Your course headline should be specific and express the course transformation that your audience desires. The course headline is the first thing your students will meet when they are searching for an outcome they desire to reach.

The template for a highly effective course transformation headline is like writing a clear learning intention. The headline highlights what the student will be able to do differently after taking the course:

Transformation Verb + Specific Content + Specific Context

Verb (What your audience will be able to do/action)
Specific Content (Your course content that will take your audience from Point A to Point B)
Specific Context (So they can get their desired solution, Point B/solution context)

Examples:

- Write the Perfect Business Plan in 8 Weeks and Unlock Your Business Success (82/72)
- Create Meaningful and Profitable Online Courses with Professional Support (74/66)
- Create Meaningful Online Courses in 8 weeks and Grow Your Passive Income (82/81)
- Craft Compelling Articles and Break into Top Media Outlets (66/43)
- Create and Launch a Product that Replaces Your One-on-One Work (68/47)

Verb	Specific Content	Context	SEO Score*
Write	The Perfect Business Plan in 8 Weeks	Unlock Your Business Success	(82/72)
Create	Meaningful and Profitable Online Courses	Professional Support	(74/66)
Create	Meaningful Online Courses in 8 weeks	Grow Your Passive Income	(82/81)
Craft	Compelling articles	Break into Top Media Outlets	(66/43)
Create and Launch	A Product	Replaces Your One-on-One Work	(68/47)

*SEO score according to Co-schedule Headline Analyzer
Ideally, you want your SEO score to be above 70
The SEO score indicates readability and how many people are searching for the specific terms per Month

Other Transformation Verbs

Other useful transformation verbs can be: *build, make, perform, apply, invent*, and *compose*.

The SOLO Taxonomy is ideal for finding ideas on action verbs.

SOLO stands for the **S**tructure of the **O**bserved **L**earning **O**utcome. The taxonomy is a means of classifying learning outcomes in terms of their complexity. It helps us to assess students' work in terms of its *quality* not of how many bits of this and of that they have got right.

WEEK 2

For more on The Solo Taxonomy, visit this link:

www.johnbiggs.com.au/academic/solo-taxonomy/

Your Specific Content and Context

Here is a method to identify the overall course transformation of your course.

My course on _____ (your course topic)

Will help _____ (your ideal audience)

Overcome_____ (possible roadblocks they may have)

By teaching them _____ (your unique transformational content)

So, they can _____ (Reach their desired solution, Point B)

Write Your Transformational Course Topic Headline

In this exercise, I encourage you to write five different headlines and test them for their SEO score.

Verb	Specific Content	Context	SEO Score*

*You can use Co-schedule Headline Analyzer on their paid plan to get SEO score and see related headlines

THE ULTIMATE COURSE CREATION GUIDE

> Free Tools:
> https://coschedule.com/headline-analyzer
> https://capitalizemytitle.com/headline-analyzer/
> https://headlines.sharethrough.com
> https://seopressor.com/blog-title-generator

Now you have a clearer idea about your transformational course topic headline. You also know how to test the SEO score of your transformational course headline to ensure your topic is something many people are searching for online.

It is important to be clear about the topic before doing market research which is your next step.

Your Market Research Worksheet

Validating your topic through market research is a great way to ensure an excellent customer-market fit for your offer.

Doing audience and market research does take some effort, but here is why it is worth your effort to do it:

- You will KNOW your course transformation topic is something many people are searching for!
- You get to REALLY know your target audience
- You will KNOW their main challenges
- You will KNOW the results they are looking for and how YOU can help them

WEEK 2

The table below has some questions for reflection and research to examine the market need.

Question for reflection and research	Yes	No	Notes
Two or more people have **paid you to solve** this problem			
A **google search** reveals blog **posts and articles** seeking to meet this need			
A search on **YouTube** shows video content on your topic			
Competitors are offering similar courses today			
Amazon has popular books on the topic			
You can find **eBooks** for sale on the topic from instructors like you			
SEO keyword search of your primary keyword reveals a **volume** of average monthly searches of more than 10.000 people			
CPC (Cost Per Click) is at least $1			

Resources for Your Keyword Research

You can use these sites to do your SEO Keyword Research and get answers about search volume and cost-per-click.

- Ubersuggest | neilpatel.com/ubersuggest/
- Wordtracker | www.wordtracker.com
- Google Keyword Planner | ads.google.com/home/tools/keyword-planner/

Record your findings in the table below. Try to look up both your primary keywords and related keywords.

Course Topic & Keywords	Search Volume Average Per Month	Cost Per Click CPC

Look for Patterns in Your Content

Here are some exercises you can do to analyze the impact of and patterns in your content and content from your competitors

- Analyze your top three pieces of content—what received the most engagements and why
- Look at top posts from competitors—why are they getting engagements?

Note your findings here:

Create a Poll on Social Media

Another way to test the waters regarding your course topic is to create a poll. Here are some examples of questions you can ask in your poll.

- "If someone did a class on X (your course topic), would you want to attend it? If no, why not?"
- "If someone created a workshop on X (your course topic), what would you want to get out of it?" (3 main outcomes to choose from and "other—leave a comment below")

Note your thoughts here: 🖎

How to Create a Poll on LinkedIn

Step 1: Create a post

Step 2: Click "Create a Poll"

THE ULTIMATE COURSE CREATION GUIDE

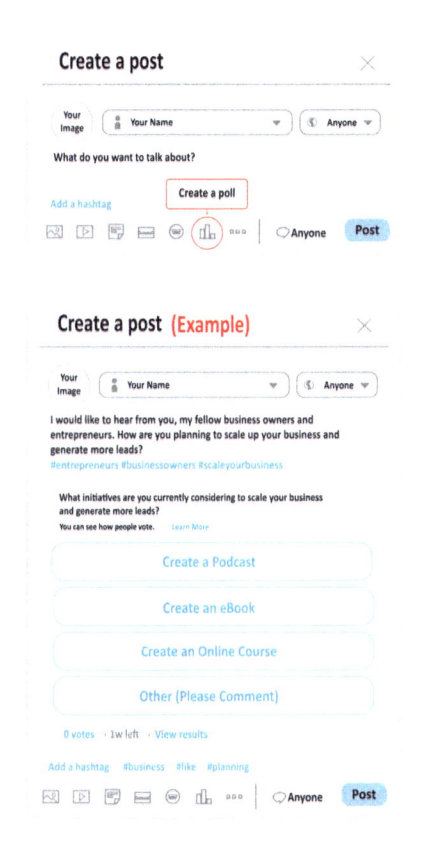

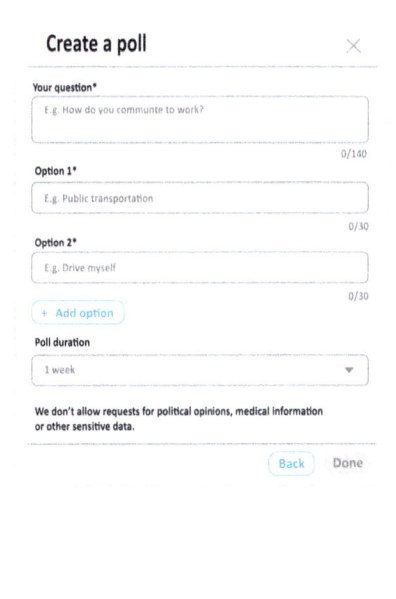

Note your findings here:

Review Testimonials

Another way to investigate what people appreciate about your expertise is to review testimonials.

Review feedback and testimonials from three people you have helped with your expertise

Look for patterns

What is your **superpower**?

> Note your findings here:

Now you may think, do I have to do all this research?

The answer is no.

Do the research that appeals to you rather than being overwhelmed by the amount of work. You can always go back and do more as you test your course and find you need more information. The purpose of the research is to get the best possible customer-market fit. And audience research is actually the best way to know exactly what your audience wants.

Audience Research Survey

Hi there, help me help you better. I'm looking to create a program for _____ (target audience) who wish to_____ (transformation your audience is looking for)! Do you have 5 minutes to answer a quick survey?

Below you will find some questions you can use for your audience research.

Audience Insight Questions

Choose the questions that work for you. Feel free to substitute these questions with others that might suit you and your audience better. You can also ask your audience what they would be willing to pay for a course on your course topic to help inform your pricing decision.

1. What current challenges are you facing when it comes to _____ (course topic)?

2. Can you tell me more about this issue? How are these challenges getting in the way of your life? How does it make you feel?

3. What is your biggest fear or concern about _____ (course transformation)?

4. What has been your biggest challenge, frustration, or problem in finding the right program to support your transition stepping into _____ (course topic)?

5. What have you tried so far to develop your skills _____ (related to the course topic/transformation)? How well did it work?

6. If you had a magic wand, what solutions would you create?

7. If you took a course on _____ (course topic), what would you like to walk away with by the end of it?

8. What would be a fair price for a course about _____ (course topic)?

9. How would your life change if you were to be successful with _____ (course transformation)?

Demographic Questions (optional)

1. **What is your age?**

    12–17 years old

    18–24 years old

    25–34 years old

    35–44 years old

    45+ years old

2. **What is your identified gender?**

    Female

    Male

    Other

    Prefer not to answer

3. **What is the highest level of education you have completed?**

    Some High School

    High School

    Bachelor's Degree

    Master's Degree

    Ph.D. or higher

    Trade School

THE ULTIMATE COURSE CREATION GUIDE

I prefer not to say

4. **What is your annual household income?**

   Less than $25,000

   $25,000 – $50,000

   $50,000 – $100,000

   $100,000 – $200,000

   More than $200,000

   Prefer not to say

May I contact you in the future regarding ✏ _____ (course topic) yes, please leave your email below.

Email: ✏ _____

Analyze the findings from your market and audience research and look for patterns.

- Are there any surprises in your findings?
- What are some key takeaways for you?

Note your findings here: ✏

🎯 Week 3: Set A Winning Competition-Based Pricing Strategy For Your Online Course

You now know **the desired transformation** your course provides to your audience. You have tested your **transformational course topic headline** and done **audience research** to test your assumptions and learn more about your audience.

This week you will learn how to **set a winning competition-based pricing strategy for your online course** and create a sustainable **financial model** to help you grow your business.

By the end of this chapter, you will know:

- How to do competitor research to find different price points and learn how you differentiate
- How to develop the financial model for your online course and your business

Remember, competition is a *good* thing. You have an audience when you find books, businesses, courses, services, and ad campaigns related to your course topic.

Competitive Research Template

Your Online Course

Competitor research will help you understand your competitors' strengths and weaknesses.

You will find inspiration for new ways to serve your customers and market your products and services. And you get to learn why customers buy from your competitors and why they buy from you. The competitor research will help you understand your business position and matchless selling point in the market.

Keyword Search

In this section, you list keywords related to your course topic, search with Google, and see similar and suggested related searches (Example: Life coaching, life coaching tools, life coaching courses . . .):

- 🖉
- 🖉
- 🖉

In the next section, you research three to five competitors with similar courses, products, and services to learn more about how you differentiate and inform your decision about pricing strategy. Use the template below for your research.

Competitor: [name]

URL:
Social links:
Key Contact:
List of comparable courses, products, and services:
What is their top content and value in what they offer?
Whom they serve/

Customer keywords:
Pricing:
Product/ Service Reviews:
What marketing strategies do they use to generate traffic and make sales?
What you now know about them:

Keywords

Strengths

Weaknesses
Inspiration related to whom you serve and how you can market your unique selling point in comparison

It is always fascinating what comes out of competitor research. One of the things I found was that not many course creators offer help with curriculum development because they don't have a background in education combined with leadership experience and know-how in business development and leadership communication in theory and practice. That was good information for me.

I suggest that you take a moment to think about your findings from your competitor research.

- What makes you special and different?
- And how does your unique offer fit with what your customers want and need?

The next exercise is designed to help you develop the financial model for your business. How does the course you are creating fit into your service offerings?

Your Financial Model

Making decisions on pricing and offers.

Examine how your unique background, experiences, passion, and talents can help your audience and set you apart from the competitors.

Think of the **$** offer as an offer that gives minimal access to your time and **$$$** the most 1-2-1 time.

Who I Serve	What Problem Do I Solve	Course Transformation
$	$$	$$$

To give you an example, I have a 3-tier offer in my course creation services.

Tier 1 $: YOU DO

You do this with general guidance. I offer a book and self-study courses with community support in this category.

Tier 2 $$: WE DO

You do this with individual guidance. In this tier, individual coaching sessions are combined with the self-study course to customize the guidance to the individual client's needs.

Tier 3 $$$: DONE FOR YOU

In this tier, I do the vast amount of the work that needs to get done in the course creation process. The client participates in weekly progress meetings.

You can see how the price of the offers reflect the different levels of access to my time and support.

Think about how your course will fit into your business model as you grow your business.

Week 4: How To Develop Your Effective Transformational Course Outline

We are now entering the content creation phase. You now know **the desired transformation** your course provides to your audience. You have tested your **transformational course topic headline.** You have done **audience research** to test your assumptions and learn more about your audience. You have **set a winning competition-based pricing strategy for your online course** and created a sustainable **financial model** for your business.

All the previous steps were part of the **idea clarification** phase of the course creation process.

This week you start developing your course content. The first step in the **content creation** phase is to build your **effective transformational course outline**.

By the end of this chapter, you will:

- Be able to explain the END GOAL of your course clearly
- Use your course mind map to help you identify the critical steps in the course transformation
- Have an effective transformational course outline that clearly defines the value your course provides to your audience and the overall steps to get there

In the content creation phase, we explore how to use different creativity tools to develop your course outline.

Your course mind map will help you identify the critical steps in the course transformation.

You might think, why do I need to use a mind map?

The thing with the mind map and other creative approaches is that the brain can be particularly logical and think in lines and boxes, especially when we have been through a lot of education. Traditional schooling trains us to be analytical and to put things in the right place. But at this point, we want to **invite nonlinear divergent thinking into the process to boost our creative problem-solving**. Because as you probably know, the first idea is rarely the best.

Please reassure your brain that we will invite the logical brain in later along the process when we're going to be more practical about organizing the ideas.

The first step in the creative process is to open up. Tell yourself that "anything is possible" no matter how stupid the logical brain might think your ideas are.

The next exercise will help you get creative and disrupt the linear, logical thinking of the brain by creating a mind map.

THE ULTIMATE COURSE CREATION GUIDE

Your Course Mind Map

Write the **end goal** of your course in the middle of the mind map.

Write the **main steps** your audience needs to take to reach the end goal in the other bubbles; then, you can **add critical elements** they need to know in the list next to the main steps.

You can use a whiteboard or pieces of paper for this exercise.

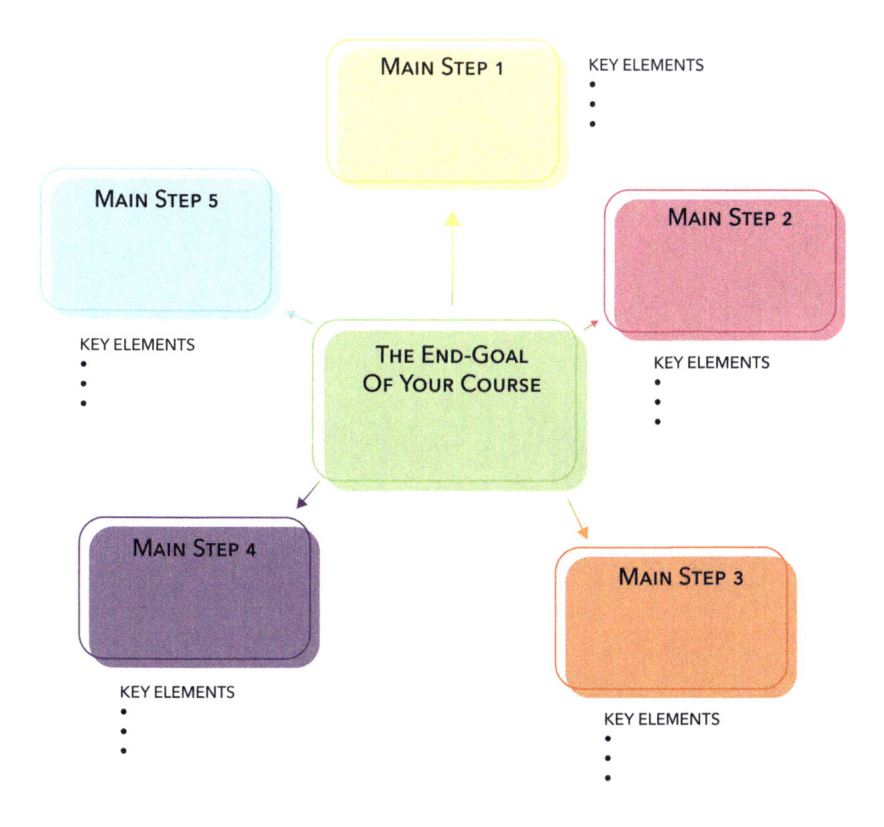

Main Step 1
KEY ELEMENTS
-
-
-

Main Step 5

KEY ELEMENTS
-
-
-

The End-Goal Of Your Course

Main Step 2

KEY ELEMENTS
-
-
-

Main Step 4

KEY ELEMENTS
-
-
-

Main Step 3

KEY ELEMENTS
-
-
-

WEEK 4

Below is an example of the early beginnings of a course mind map. The mind map is for a course about how to guide people through organizational change as a manager.

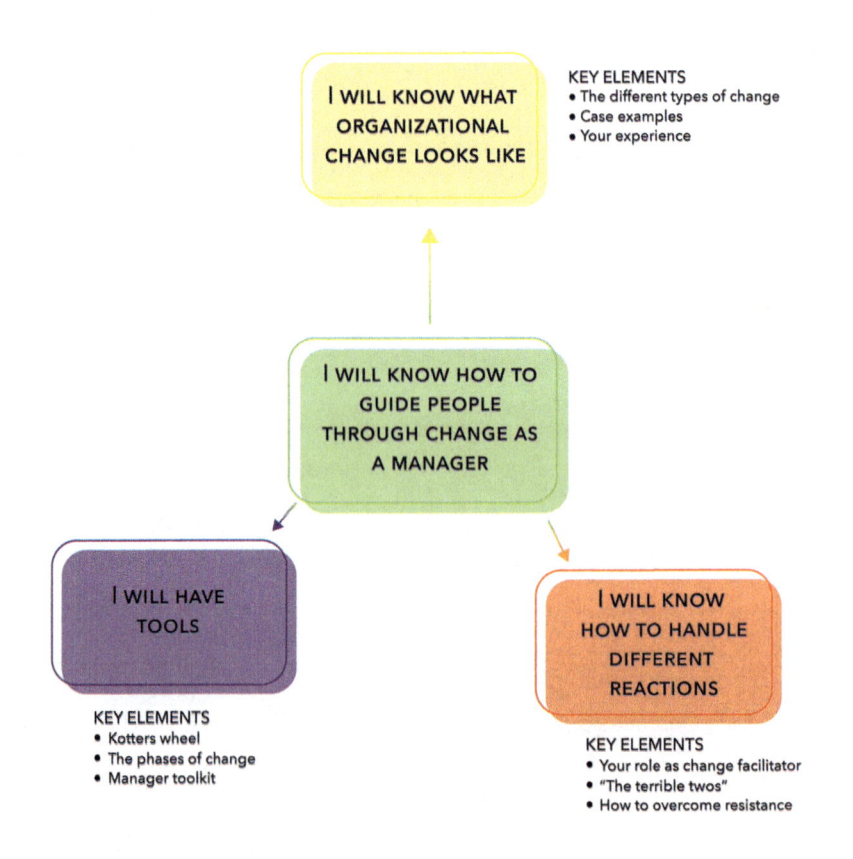

I WILL KNOW WHAT ORGANIZATIONAL CHANGE LOOKS LIKE

KEY ELEMENTS
- The different types of change
- Case examples
- Your experience

I WILL KNOW HOW TO GUIDE PEOPLE THROUGH CHANGE AS A MANAGER

I WILL HAVE TOOLS

KEY ELEMENTS
- Kotters wheel
- The phases of change
- Manager toolkit

I WILL KNOW HOW TO HANDLE DIFFERENT REACTIONS

KEY ELEMENTS
- Your role as change facilitator
- "The terrible twos"
- How to overcome resistance

The next exercise will help you write your effective transformational course outline. In the outline, you can use the key steps you identified in your mind map.

The key purpose of the course outline is to define the value your course provides to your audience. **When you're really clear on what your audience wants, you can define and develop the content for the steps that will help them get there.**

Your Course Outline Worksheet

Fill out the blank spaces in the worksheet with the value of your course, the end goal for your audience, and the main steps to reach the end goal of the course.

Your task	Goal	Notes
Define your course value	Get clear on your audience's wants and how you will help them get there. What is the value of the transformation you provide for your audience?	Revisit questions in the discovery questionnaire about course value. Sum up the results from your research.
The value of my course	✏️	✏️
Create your course outline	Clarify the end goal of the course. What will the audience be able to do differently after following the steps and guidance in your class?	For the course to be practical and effective, focus on helping your audience get the desired result (rather than share everything you know).
	Reverse engineering. Define the steps they need to take to reach the end goal. Steps – tools – tasks – exercises/ activities.	Specifics are popular: • Blueprints • Templates • Step-by-step guides • Cheat-sheets • Swipe files

WEEK 4

Create your course outline	Remember, too much content will overwhelm your audience. Focus on the incremental, step-by-step result that helps your audience solve their big problem. How will they know they have reached the end goal?		
The end goal of my course	✏️		✏️
Main step 1	✏️		✏️
Main step 2	✏️		✏️
Main step 3	✏️		✏️
Main step 4	✏️		✏️
Main step 5	✏️		✏️
Main step 6	✏️		✏️

Let me give you an example of how you can use this worksheet from my course. My course value is that my students will be able to grow their business with their own online course. My students also get to share their passion and unique knowledge and help more people reach their goals and generate passive income by having an online course as part of their business.

These values are in line with my core belief that learning is the pathway to freedom.

The end goal in my course is for my students to grow their business by having a course of their own, which is why I have included the steps in this course based on my experience of what works when creating meaningful and profitable online courses.

Then I reverse engineered the process with the steps I know are needed to make an online program including the steps, tools, tasks, exercises, and activities.

Another component to keep in mind is to **look at your content through the eyes of your students**. A way to do that is to have interactions with your students. Ask questions to examine their understanding and if there are things you need to explain better.

Remember that too much content will overwhelm your audience.

Focus on incremental, step-by-step results to help your audience solve their "big" problem. Specifics like blueprints, templates, step-by-step guides, cheat sheets, and swipe files are popular.

Keep in mind how your students will know the moment they have reached the end goal. What signs can you provide for them to know that they're on the right path? Think of the signs along a treasure map that mark the milestones.

Week 5: How To Create A Simple And Effective Storyboard For Your Online Course

We are now diving further into the course content. The **storyboard** will help you organize your content. For each lesson, start thinking about the value of the lesson, the **WHY**. Then you teach them what they need to **KNOW** to learn this element that is part of their journey toward the end goal. Then you give them a tool on **HOW** to implement the solution. And then think about how you can get them to **APPLY** their new knowledge and share.

By the end of this chapter, you will:

- Know how to create a storyboard and have seen an example of how to fill out a storyboard
- Have completed a storyboard with keywords for each module and lesson in your course

Keep it simple!

Before we dive into the exercises in this chapter, think about something that you are really good at today. It can be cooking, a sport, playing an instrument. Now think back to the beginning when you were completely new at this thing you are good at today.

- Think about what helped you learn in the beginning? What type of feedback did you need when you were completely new?

- And then later, as you became better? How were you learning? What type of feedback did you need? And what helped you evolve past the intermediate level of understanding?
- Now that you're an expert, and genuinely good at whatever you're good at, what feedback do you seek?

Remembering your own experience learning something new will help you keep it simple for your students. A helpful visual when planning your content is to think about creating hooks to help your students build the new knowledge onto knowledge they already possess. Also think about how your students can apply the new knowledge in exercises and questions for reflection to help them integrate what they are learning.

Making the learning process easier

The solo taxonomy by Biggs and Collis was developed through describing and analyzing how people actually learn. The first step in any learning, no matter what we're learning, is the pre-structural step. This is the step before I start learning. In this phase, I don't know. I have no idea.

Let me give you an example. This summer I started learning how to play golf. My first time on the greens, I had absolutely no idea how to play. I didn't know how to hold the club or strike the ball. My first attempts resulted in big holes in the grass.

The next step of the learning process is to get an idea of what I'm learning.

In my example my husband showed me a YouTube video where a professional golfer breaks down each component of the swing, and what goes into the swing in order to hit the ball. After I saw that, I had an idea about how I could approach the swing.

The next phase after that is trying to actually define the motion I was watching and try to replicate that. At this phase of the learning process, I have a couple of ideas, but I'm still in the early phase of learning. You can call it "superficial" learning. To help me develop more proficiency I am currently taking lessons from a golf pro.

The next deeper phase of the learning process can begin once the basic scaffold is in place. At this point I can begin to apply the new knowledge on a more consistent basis.

I'm not there yet, when it comes to golfing.

The last phase of the learning process is when we are able to apply the knowledge that we have gained in a new context independently. That's the practical application goal of any learning. This shows "in-depth" learning.

When we are creating online courses, we can think about how we can provide cycles of continuous learning like a spiral where each new component your students are learning builds on the previous. And if possible, think about how you can provide feedback loops, either in group or individual settings, that can be part of the upsell strategy for growing your business.

What Is A Content Storyboard?

The purpose of the storyboard is to outline a content sketch for each lesson in each module or chapter of your online course. Remember that your end goal is like the trunk of the tree. The modules or chapters are the main branches. And the lessons are the twigs.

The structure of your course is meant to provide your clients a high-impact "HOW TO" to help them reach their end goal.

WEEK 5

Look at the course through your students' eyes to help them get the transformation they desire and achieve their Point B.

- What does the learning process look like when you look through the eyes of your students?

The storyboard defines the steps your audience needs to take to reach the end goal and tools they can apply (blueprints, templates, step-by-step guides, cheat sheets, swipe files)—exercises/activities.

All modules and the lessons in each module follow the same basic outline with an overall **GOAL**, title (SEO), why (value), what (know), how (tools), and try (apply). The purpose is to get your audience to see the value—the **WHY**. Teach them what they need to **KNOW** to figure out how to implement. Give them a tool on **HOW** to implement the solution. And finally, get them to **APPLY** the new knowledge and share.

The outline for each lesson follows the same structure:

- **Intro**—goal/learning intention "after this module, my students will be able to . . ."
- **Why**—value
- **What**—describe and share essential knowledge needed to understand
- **How**—relate, a tool on how to implement the solution to reach the goal
- **Apply/Call to Action**—apply the new knowledge
- **Outro**

You can have one or more lessons per chapter or module. Think of each lesson as one type of instruction (video, text, assignment, quiz, etc.).

THE ULTIMATE COURSE CREATION GUIDE   41

Check out the link below to see an example of a course structure with chapter headlines and individual lessons on how to write great copy people love to read for inspiration:

https://courses.sophiehhiggins.com/courses/
how-to-write-great-copy-people-love-to-read

Chapter	Course Overview
1	**Welcome To How To Write Great Content People Actually Love To Read**
	🎥 Why writing great content people love to read is important
2	**Module 1: How To Choose A Winning Topic That Solves Your Clients Problem**
	🎥 How To Research And Test Your Ideas With Your Ideal Client Avatar
	🎥 What Is Your Powerful Solution To Your Clients Problem?
	📋 Questions about your client survey
3	**Module 2: How To Generate And Structure Your Great Content Ideas**
	🎥 3 Different Creative Methods To Generate Innovative Ideas [Video icon] How To Structure Your Copy For Success
	⬇️ Download Your Structure Template

4	**Module 3: How To Make A Captivating Headline And Lead Using Seo Keywords**
	🎥 Get A Catchy Headline Template
	🎥 A Powerful Method To Test Your Headline And Lead
	🎥 How To Test Headline And SEO Keywords
	⬇ Get Your Headline Template & Method To Test Your Headline And Lead
5	**Module 4: Get A Powerful Template To Follow To Write The Best Content**
	🎥 Get A Template To Write Articles People Love To Read
	⬇ Daily Compelling Content Template
6	**Module 5: How To Use Storytelling To Gain Your Readers Attention**
	🎥 How To Use Storytelling To Illustrate The Benefits Of Your Business

Storyboard Example

Here you find an example of a partially filled storyboard from the course that goes with this book.

THE ULTIMATE COURSE CREATION GUIDE

What is the focus in each step towards reaching the end goal	Module 1	Module 2	Module 3	Module 4
🎯 **GOAL**	Find your unique combination of talents to serve your audience in your course	Create and test the irresistible course offer	Set the right competition-based pricing strategy	Develop your course outline
🔍 **Title (SEO)**	How To Easily Find Your Really Helpful Online Education Topic!	How To Write And Test Your Irresistible Online Course Offer	Set A Winning Competition-Based Pricing Strategy For Your Online Course	How To Develop Your Effective Transformational Course Outline
❗ **WHY/ VALUE**	It will set you apart when you find how you are unique, who you serve and how it matches with the transformation your audience desires.	An SEO strong headline and a topic people are searching for is vital for people to find and want your offer and course transformation.	In creating a course that will sell, it is essential to know what your competitors are asking for a similar course.	...

WEEK 5

🔍 **WHAT they NEED to KNOW to implement goal**	Identify your unique combination of skills, talent, background, and experience and how you solved a problem and reached point B.	How to write your hot transformational course topic headline How to test your course headline and make sure your topic is something many people are searching for How to do audience research to test your assumptions about your audience and the outcome they desire	...
✂ **HOW/TOOL to implement new learning**	Your Unique Course Transformation Worksheet	Your Transformational Course Topic Headline Worksheet	

THE ULTIMATE COURSE CREATION GUIDE

← APPLY/ CTA Exercise to try (and share) Think about your Audience - Their Burning Desire and How you will help them get from POINT A to POINT B

After the overall outline is in place, you can make a visual/text storyboard or slides with talking points for each video in more detail.

Your Content Storyboard

What is the focus in each step towards reaching the end goal	Module 1	Module 2	Module 3	Module 4
🎯 GOAL				
🔍 Title (SEO)				
❓ WHY/VALUE				
🔑 WHAT they NEED to KNOW to implement goal				
🔧 HOW/TOOL to APPLY new learning				
← TRY/CTA Exercise to Implement (and share)				

Summing up all modules, and all lessons in each module follow the same basic outline. There is an overall **goal** with the module and the lessons to help overcome an obstacle and get one step closer to the end goal and the desired outcome.

The **SEO** title is important for the search engines to grow the number of organic impressions.

In each module and lesson, you want to explain **why** it is important to complete this step. **What** is it your students need to know, to overcome this obstacle, or to accomplish this step, and then what tool can you give them for **how** to do it, and an exercise that helps them **apply** this new tool for themselves.

The reason for this structure is that it will help your students through the steps of the learning process. This structure guides the learner to take those steps in bite-size pieces. It gets your students to see the value, the why. When you are learning something new, it is motivating when you know why you are learning it. The structure also reminds you to teach them what they need to know and how to take the step.

You help your students get the main ideas of what they need to know, and then you give them tools they need to help them implement the solution, and how to apply it. At the end of each lesson, help your students apply their new knowledge and share it. The reason why it is important to help your students apply what they are learning is because when they apply new knowledge it helps them deepen their learning and it helps their ability to apply the new knowledge independently and in new contexts.

This also helps your students become free of you, so they don't have to keep relying on you as a crutch. **You want to empower people to be free.**

Week 6: Effectively Organize Your Online Course In Your Learning Management Platform

In the previous chapter, you used the storyboard template to develop the content structure of your course. This week is the time to prepare your learning program **for launch** in your **learning management platform**.

You will have several learning management systems to choose from, and maybe you have one working for you already. No matter what, the considerations and setup are similar.

I recommend **Thinkific** because it is easy to use and has excellent support. Thinkific also allows for live Zoom integration, which is helpful in your beta testing process. Here is a <u>link</u> to their free basic plan to test the platform for yourself. The Zoom integration comes with their Pro Plan

This chapter will help you organize your **course structure** with welcome modules, lessons with videos, live calls, and supporting learning content such as quizzes, assignments, downloadable templates, pdf, etc.

WEEK 6

By the end of this chapter, you will:

- See several examples of how to create a course structure in your learning management platform for inspiration
- Set up your course structure from your storyboard into your learning management platform
- Use the template to write the welcome for each module to create an engaging and empowering learning experience

Follow this link to get the free plan at *Thinkific*.

Your Course Structure Guide

It is time to start building the actual course structure in the learning management platform or Learning Management System (LMS) you have chosen.

In this guide, I will show you examples to help you set up your course structure in your LMS:

1. What the structure looks like from the backend of the LMS
2. How you can structure the content of each module
3. How to support the learning journey with a module introduction in the LMS

THE ULTIMATE COURSE CREATION GUIDE 51

AD 1. What the structure looks like from the backend of the LMS

Below is an example of the structure from the backend of the LMS (Thinkific).

When you sign in to your LMS, you will get into a dashboard, which will look similar to this.

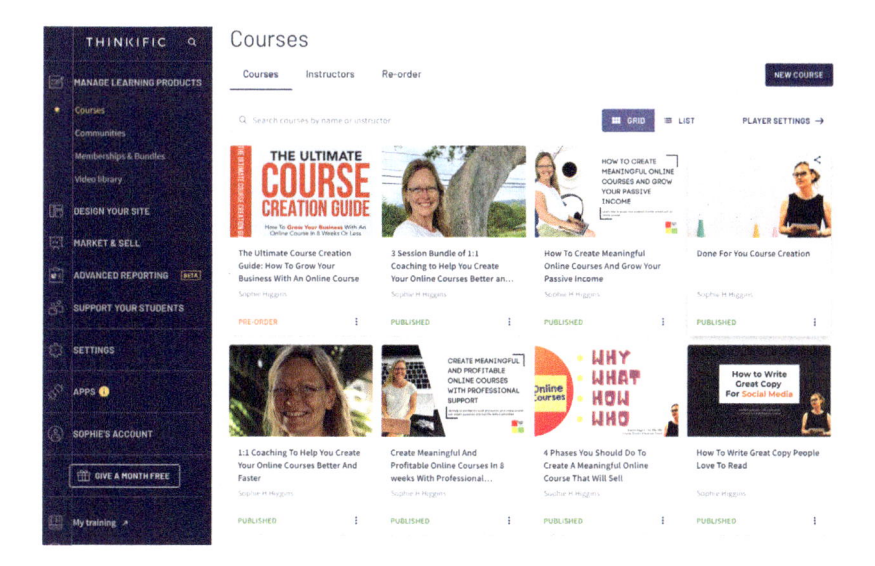

The next step is creating or editing a course you have started. When you click on the course, you get to the **course builder**. The course builder typically appears in the image below with the modules (in this course, structured by weeks) and the lessons under each module.

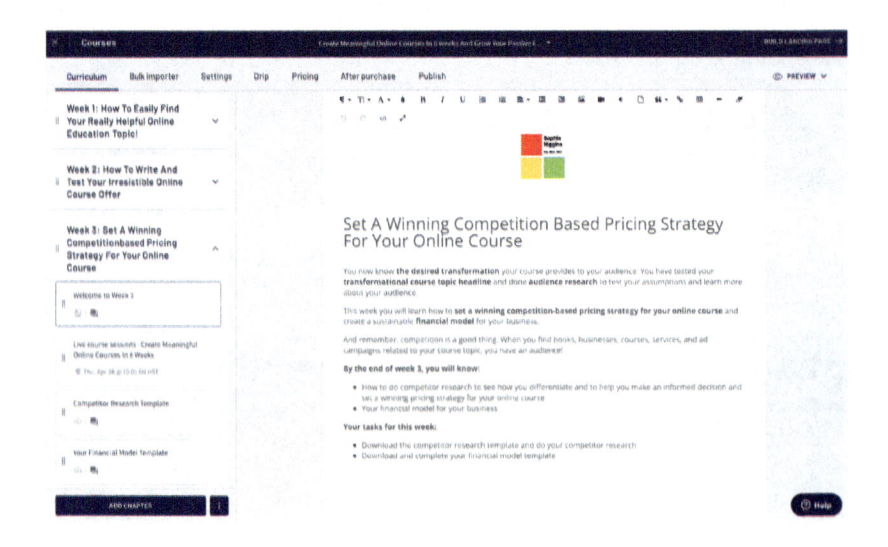

AD 2. How to structure the content of each module

You can use the following structure to organize the content from your storyboard into the learning management platform.

A rule of thumb is to have one major learning goal per module or chapter that helps your students get from point A to point B.

THE ULTIMATE COURSE CREATION GUIDE

Often you will have more than one lesson per module. Each lesson will help your students step by step accomplish the milestone for that module covering elements like:

- An introduction with the milestone, the goal, and the *why*
- The *what*
- The *how*
- The *apply*

The lesson types include instructional videos, learning support, student submissions, quizzes, etc.

The lesson formats include video (talking-head style, screencasting, presentation of slide decks, transcripts), audio, live interactive session, text, image, downloads, quizzes, assignments, surveys, and community.

A general guideline for video content is to keep premade videos simple, short, and to the point (5-15 minutes per video or even shorter).

The **structure** for a welcome module can look like this:

Lesson Name	Lesson Type	Lesson Format
Welcome from your instructor	Introduction lesson (Why the course topic and why you can help your audience get the transformation they desire)	Text and video
Before we begin	Student submission	Survey
Your discovery questionnaire	Questions to support learning	Word download

WEEK 6

Here is an example of what a module structure can look like:

Lesson Name	Lesson Type	Lesson Format
Week 2 - Overview and download	Introduction to week 2 and templates	Text and download
Week 2 - Live session	Live session/Lesson	Zoom/video replay
Example	Lesson and examples	Video and PDF download
Worksheet	Template to support learning	Word download
Checklist	Student submission	Quiz

Lesson Name	Lesson Type	Lesson Format
Week 4: How to Develop Your Effective Transformational Course Outline	Chapter title	SEO tested headline
Welcome to Week 4	Introduction to week 4 and templates	Text and Download
Welcome To The Content Creation Phase And Understand The Learning Process To Develop Your Transformational Course Outline	Lesson and examples	Video
How To Use A Mind Map To Effectively Identify The Steps in Your Course Outline	Lesson and examples	Video
Your Course Mind Map	Template to support learning	PDF download (fillable)
How To Create Your Effective Course Outline	Lesson and examples	Video
Course Outline Worksheet	Template to support learning	Word document

AD 3. How to support the learning journey with a module introduction in the LMS

Here you will find an example of how you can support the learning journey for the student by writing an introduction to each module.

The structure for module introductions can look like this:

Welcome to Week X
[Brief introduction to the goal and the why]
In this week...[Brief introduction to the what and how]
You will use... [Brief introduction to the apply]

By the end of Week X, you will have:
- [Outcome X]
- [Outcome Y]
- [Outcome Z]

Your tasks for this week:
- Participate in the live session or watch the replay
- Download and complete the Worksheet
- Download and review [the example...]
- Test your [new knowledge] in the Quiz

Example Module Introduction

Here is a case study example from one of my clients you can use for inspiration.

> **Welcome to Week 1** 🎉
> Knowing why you are in business and who you serve is the first important step in building a successful business. The key is to get the right product or service with the best possible benefits to the right people and at the right time and place.
>
> We struggled at the beginning of building our two successful businesses: "We wanted to help everyone." Finding a niche and identifying a target market was essential and helped us get clients more efficiently. The other area was the struggle with finances and getting enough working capital. Maybe you recognize this. Don't worry. We will cover all these areas in this course.
>
> This week, we focus on how you can find an opening or unmet need within a market and then fill it rather than try and push in your product or service. It's much easier to satisfy a need than to create one and convince people they should spend money on it.
>
> This week, we start with getting clear on your offer and your target market; to do so, we have to be ready to do some thinking and research.
>
> **By the end of Week 1, you will have listed:**
> - Your product or services
> - The benefits or value your product or services provide to your customers
> - Your target markets
> - Your referral sources (where you get in touch with your customers)
>
> **Your tasks for this week:**
> - Participate in the live session or watch the replay
> - Download and complete the Product Service Benefit Target Market RS Worksheet

THE ULTIMATE COURSE CREATION GUIDE

The following **course setup checklist** will help you make sure you have all the elements in place for your online course.

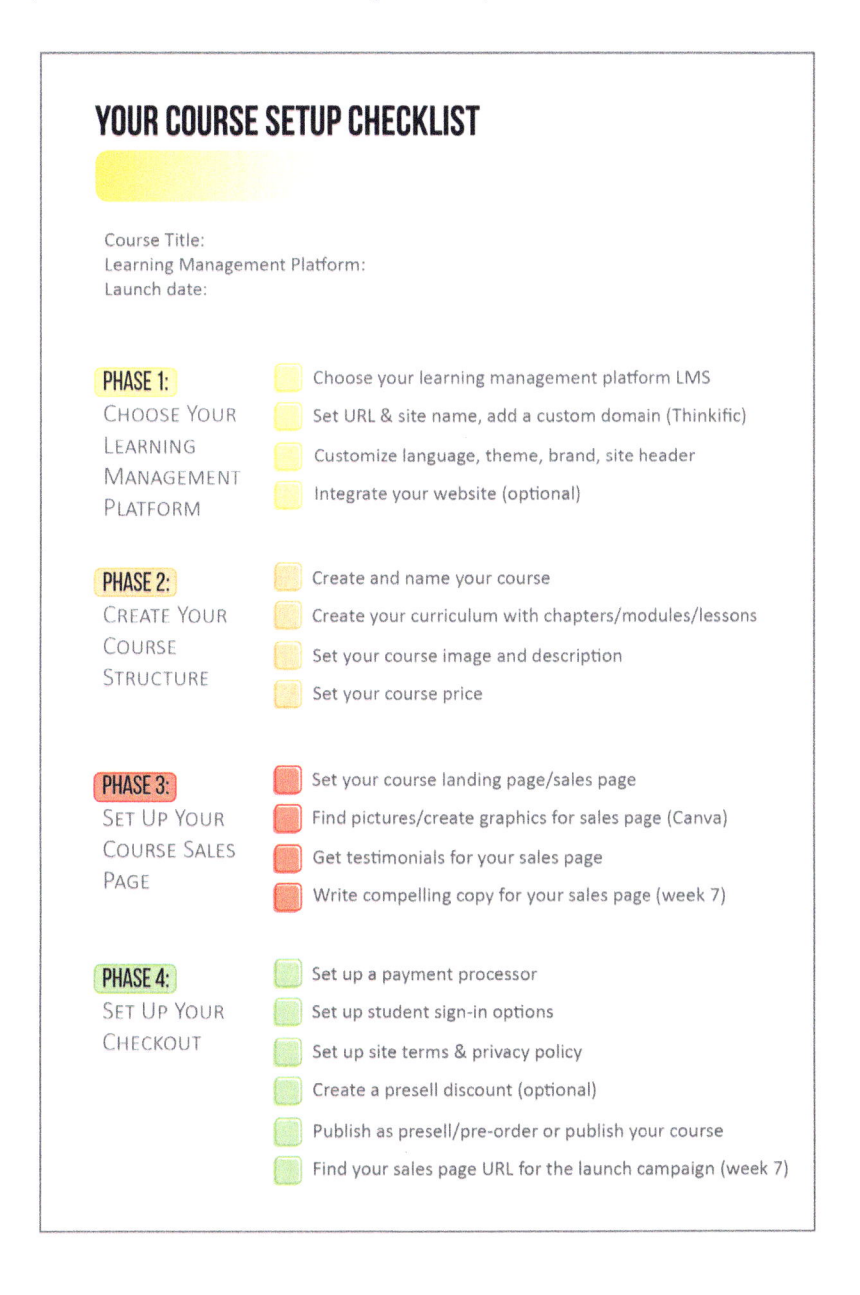

YOUR COURSE SETUP CHECKLIST

Course Title:
Learning Management Platform:
Launch date:

PHASE 1:
CHOOSE YOUR LEARNING MANAGEMENT PLATFORM

- ☐ Choose your learning management platform LMS
- ☐ Set URL & site name, add a custom domain (Thinkific)
- ☐ Customize language, theme, brand, site header
- ☐ Integrate your website (optional)

PHASE 2:
CREATE YOUR COURSE STRUCTURE

- ☐ Create and name your course
- ☐ Create your curriculum with chapters/modules/lessons
- ☐ Set your course image and description
- ☐ Set your course price

PHASE 3:
SET UP YOUR COURSE SALES PAGE

- ☐ Set up your course landing page/sales page
- ☐ Find pictures/create graphics for sales page (Canva)
- ☐ Get testimonials for your sales page
- ☐ Write compelling copy for your sales page (week 7)

PHASE 4:
SET UP YOUR CHECKOUT

- ☐ Set up a payment processor
- ☐ Set up student sign-in options
- ☐ Set up site terms & privacy policy
- ☐ Create a presell discount (optional)
- ☐ Publish as presell/pre-order or publish your course
- ☐ Find your sales page URL for the launch campaign (week 7)

Week 7: Rig Your Online Course Launch Strategy With Exciting And Effective Sales Copy

Why is this important?

Well, no customers, no money.

And on top of that, you will have spent a lot of time and a lot of wasted effort.

That is why getting people to enroll in your course is imperative to launch your online course successfully.

The main thing for people to register for your program is that **they need to know about you and your services.**

One of the main ingredients in catching people's attention is writing compelling and persuasive sales copy and having an effective launch schedule to plan how to put your content in front of the right people at the right time.

This week you will learn to rig your online course launch strategy with compelling sales copy.

By the end of this chapter, you will:

- Know how to write a compelling sales page for your online course to get it ready for presale
- Develop a launch strategy and have your launch schedule prepared for a magnetic customer experience funnel
- Adjust the content in the swipe file for your email campaign to match your online course

Copy for the Sales Page

You can check out the following examples of sales pages for inspiration:

- https://courses.sophiehhiggins.com/courses/Create-Meaningful-Online-Courses-And-Grow-Passive-Income
- https://courses.sophiehhiggins.com/courses/how-to-write-great-copy-people-love-to-read
- https://courses.seriousbusinesssolutions.info/courses/Write-Your-Business-Plan
- https://rozhuang-masterclass.thinkific.com/courses/Master-of-the-Basic

Here is a client case study example of a sales page for inspiration.

THE ULTIMATE COURSE CREATION GUIDE

Follow the link to the sales page above. The link will take you the sales page I wrote for Roz Huang and her Master of the Business Basics leadership course. Please notice the embedded videos on the sales page as an example of how you can integrate both professional and handheld videos in your marketing material to give your audience a professional versus a more intimate, personalized experience or use both to **utilize all three rhetorical appeals on your sales page: ethos, pathos and logos**.

Ethos is building your credibility. Testimonials are ways to boost your credibility. Pathos appeals to the emotions of your audience. You appeal to people's emotions when you talk about their fears and desires and how you can help them overcome their current obstacles. Logos is the appeal to reason and logic. You can appeal to people's logic when you talk about features, benefits, and bonuses. A good sales page includes all three types of rhetorical appeals.

Another point that is important to know is that we buy with our emotions and then we rationalize and justify the purchase with our reason. That is also why you will find that one of the first elements on most sales pages is the PAS story (problems, agitate, solve) that is filled with emotional appeal. See if you can identify the appeal to people's emotions in the example of the PAS story below.

Here is a case study to illustrate how you can write your sales page.

WEEK 7

The example is from the sales page I wrote for Joann Seery and her course Write the Perfect Business Plan in 8 Weeks and Unlock Your Business Success.

Working title:

Example working title: Plan for Success - Write Your Business Plan (64/39 SEO)

Alternative titles:

Example alternative titles
- Write Your Business Plan to Ensure Your Business Success (69/60)
- Write the Perfect Business Plan Step-by-Step in 8 Weeks (79/74)
- Write the Perfect Business Plan in 8 Weeks (70/63)
- Write the Perfect Business Plan in 8 Weeks And Unlock Your Business Success (82/72)

SEO testing of the headline with Co-Schedule Headline Analyzer https://headlines.coschedule.com

Course Image

You can find great free images at https://unsplash.com

Course Description

Example course description
Did you know that most new businesses fail because they lack or have an inadequate business plan? This course will guide you in writing a perfect business plan and achieving business success

THE ULTIMATE COURSE CREATION GUIDE

CTA – Call to Action
Enroll today

PAS Story
　　　　　　Problem - What's the Problem?
　　Agitate - What are the consequences of not solving this problem?
　　　　Solve - What's your unique solution to this problem?

Example PAS Story
Did you know that 20% of all new businesses fail during the first two years of being in business? And did you know that only 25% of new companies make it to 15 years or more? According to the U.S. Bureau of Labor Statistics (BLS), companies fail because they don't have the proper planning, funding, or flexibility. We at Serious Business Solutions are passionate about helping businesses be successful. We have helped 1000s of business owners over the last 25 years to be successful by assisting them step-by-step in creating a simple business plan. We know that these business plans have helped them be successful in the long run. We even got an award for helping more businesses get business loans than the established banks!
And we want to help you be successful in business too!

Course Introduction
All the need-to-know details:

Example of Course Introduction
Write The Perfect Business Plan In 8 Weeks is for ambitious and early-phase small business owners or those that have already launched a business but need to create a business plan to support their strategic growth or secure financing. Through eight weeks of online live sessions and business coaching, you will learn how to manage, market, and finance your business while creating a simple and solid business plan. You get all the templates you need and step-by-step guidance throughout this comprehensive course to plan for your business to succeed.

CTA – Call to Action
Save your seat

Social Proof

Here's what people say about us:
"Quote"—Name
"Quote"—Name
"Quote"—Name

> ❝

Sophie Higgins has created a content rich online course that teaches business owners step by step how to create powerful copy to gain more business. Each module is broken down into bite size chunks to make it easy to watch and implement the information. I highly recommend this course!

★★★★★

- Dr. Lisa Thompson, Best-Selling Author, Speaker, Galactic Ambassador, and Intuitive Transformational Coach

THE ULTIMATE COURSE CREATION GUIDE

Course Outcomes

List the major outcomes and milestones your students can expect to reach by the end of your course. Use the list to convince your audience that your course can help them get the desired outcome. Answer the question in their mind: what's in it for me?

Example Course Outcomes

Here is what you will get in the course
Write The Perfect Business Plan In 8 Weeks And Unlock Your Business Success!

In this course, released over 8 weeks, you get live instruction, downloadable tools, templates, exercises, and quizzes to help you to write your own perfect business plan step-by-step while you take the course.

8 Course Modules
These 8 modules walk you through writing your business plan step-by-step and how plan for success.

Tools & Templates
Downloadable templates you can apply to effectively write your own solid business plan to support your strategic growth.

Pricing Strategy
Learn how to conduct competitor and market research to set the right pricing strategy for your service or product.

Business Formation
Gain knowledge and support for how to choose the right business formation and the associated tax implications.

Financial Modeling
Your financial plan will show you how much is needed to run your business, pay your bills, pay yourself, and invest in marketing.

SWOT Analysis
Complete a SWOT (Strengths, Weaknesses, Opportunities, Threats) analysis to include in your operational plan.

Understand Your Why
Get clear focus in your mission statement and your product or service description to help steer your business through highs and lows.

Marketing Plans
Learn to create a marketing plan to help you prioritize and make cost-effective choices to attract the right people at the right cost.

Confidence In Yourself
Build the confidence that you have all the planning in place to grow your business for success.

WEEK 7

Bonus Material
Bonuses when you join now!
Here you can write the bonuses and resources to help handle objections, remove roadblocks, and make your audience feel lucky.

Meet your instructor
Write about yourself as an instructor. Remember to give people an opportunity to relate to you and to build trust that you have walked the path before them from Point A to Point B.

Price
You can consider a regular price, a monthly subscription, and possibly a discounted presell price for your beta test with live sessions.

Regular price: $

Discounted (presell) price (example 50% off):

Countdown timer (optional)
Indicate how long your students must purchase and enroll in your presell course.

Example Count-down timer
Pre-orders are closing soon! Save your seat and get XX% off the total price of this course by enrolling today.
This program begins on X (date).

THE ULTIMATE COURSE CREATION GUIDE

Guarantee seal (optional)
Remember to include the timeframe and guidelines of your money-back guarantee.

Example 100% Satisfaction Guarantee for 30 days
Join our course Write The Perfect Business Plan In 8 Weeks And Unlock Your Business Success and get reassurance that if the course doesn't work for you, you have 30 days to request your money back with no questions asked. Although all our clients have loved how we have helped them write their business plans so far, we want to ensure you get value for your money and find our product helpful.

CTA – Call to Action
Enroll today

FAQs
Answer frequently asked questions that your audience may have.

FAQ Example
1. How long do I have access to the course content?
Participants have unlimited lifetime access to the course content (all modules, videos, and tools).

2. What if I cannot make one or more of the scheduled live online sessions?
The live sessions will be recorded on video and uploaded to that week's module on the day of the call. You can then watch or revisit the session at your leisure.

3. What if I cannot work on writing my business plan while the course content is being released?
No worries. You will have lifetime access to all the modules and material. It is designed in a sequence to work at your own pace. You can pause or revisit the program anytime.

4. What if I have questions, I want to ask the instructor?
At the end of each live call, there will be time for Q&A

Below you will find a template for a launch schedule. The launch schedule will help you plan your launch campaign and schedule your emails to get people from your email list to sign up for your course.

Launch schedule template

Week 1 – Nurture (2 emails and posts)
- Email 1 - Launch Primer
- Wait two days
- Email 2 - Pre-Launch Invitation
- Wait two days

Week 2 – Sales (4 emails and posts)
- Email 3 - Launch Day and Limited Time Offer
- Wait one day
- Email 4 - Introducing the Problem
- Wait one day
- Email 5 - Introducing the Solution
- Wait one day
- Email 6 - The Benefit of Solving the Problem

Week 3 – Sale closing (1 email/post and three count-down email/posts)
- Email 7 - Social Proof + FOMO (Fear of missing out)
- Email 8 – 48 hours left
- Email 9 – 24 hours left
- Email 10 – last chance

The email sequence in the launch schedule will give you enough time to your audience to become aware of your offer, see the benefit of solving the problem, and want to join you in getting the solution.

THE ULTIMATE COURSE CREATION GUIDE

The swipe copy below is an example of how you can write emails for your email campaign. You just need to adjust for your topic.

Launch Schedule for Your Online Course—Email Campaign and Social Posts

Email #	Week	Topic	Headline	Copy	Notes
1	Nurture	Primer	I'm so excited! My new course is almost ready for you!	Hey, [First Name], I just wanted to give you some advanced notice that I'm building something new for you and it's coming soon! You'll be one of the first to get early access to this course that launches on DATE. Stay tuned for an email with more details. Thanks, NAME P.S. If you're eager to find out more, reply to MAIL and tell me about your biggest challenge with COURSE TOPIC	Course in draft - sales page set up
2	Nurture	Pre-Launch Invite	It's almost ready ... Enroll early for a special discount	Hey, [First Name], I just wanted to give you some advanced notice that I'm about to launch a brand-new course called COURSE NAME. In this 8-week course, you'll be learning everything you need to know to COURSE OUTCOME. I can't wait to see what you think. As a special bonus for those interested, everyone who signs up for the course before DATE will receive a 50% discount as a thank you for your anticipation! And you'll be the first to know when the course goes live! Join the waiting list here! LINK There are LIMITED spots! So, Sign up soon!	

WEEK 7

Get access to the launch schedule and the swipe file with copy for an email campaign with ten emails by enrolling in the course with in-depth explanations and examples of how to take each step. If you follow the link here in this book, you get 50 percent off the regular course price.

https://courses.sophiehhiggins.com/courses/Create-Meaningful-Online-Courses-And-Grow-Passive-Income?coupon=ultimateguide

Week 8: How To Easily Plan, Run, And Record Your Live Sessions And Prepare For Better Relaunch

The advantages of making your initial course launch a **live launch** are many. You get to test the **customer-market fit** and actual interest in your online course topic before spending a lot of additional time recording your videos.

You also get to collect **feedback** and make improvements for a **better relaunch** while your brain is still open for input because your brain knows that it is a "work in progress." You get to collect **testimonials** from people who have been through your course that you can use to make your relaunch sales page, and **Webinar Sales Funnel** even more persuasive.

And you get to record your live calls and turn parts of these live sessions into videos you can use in your evergreen product.

By the end this chapter, you will:

- Know how to plan, run, and record your live sessions using presentations slides or talking points
- Learn how to collect feedback and use the input to prepare for a better relaunch
- Prepare for a better relaunch with a Webinar Sales Funnel

Guide To Plan And Run Live Lessons

Here are three reasons why it is a great idea to beta test your online course because it will end up saving you time and money:

1. When you beta test your course, you will get direct hard evidence from your audience on whether or not you have a potential winning course topic. If people sign up, great! If they don't, you can make your adjustments to ensure a better customer-market fit before having spent hours and hours filming and editing.

2. When you beta test, you don't have to have all the videos of your course ready upfront. With a live test launch, you can record while presenting. You can edit and use this live footage as part of your evergreen course product.

3. When you beta test, your brain is open to feedback because it knows it still is a "work in progress." You can make changes based on the questions and feedback you receive from your participants. Doing this will give you a clearer idea of where you need to adjust your content and get testimonials for your relaunch.

https://sophiehhiggins.com/2022/04/07/3-reasons-why-you-should-bother-to-beta-test-your-online-course

The learning process

The infographic shows the phases in the learning process. When we are learning something new, we first need to build knowledge. We can start making meaning and find connections when we have a basic understanding. When we can apply our new knowledge, we develop deeper learning. If we discover we need to know more, we build new knowledge because knowledge-building is an iterative process.

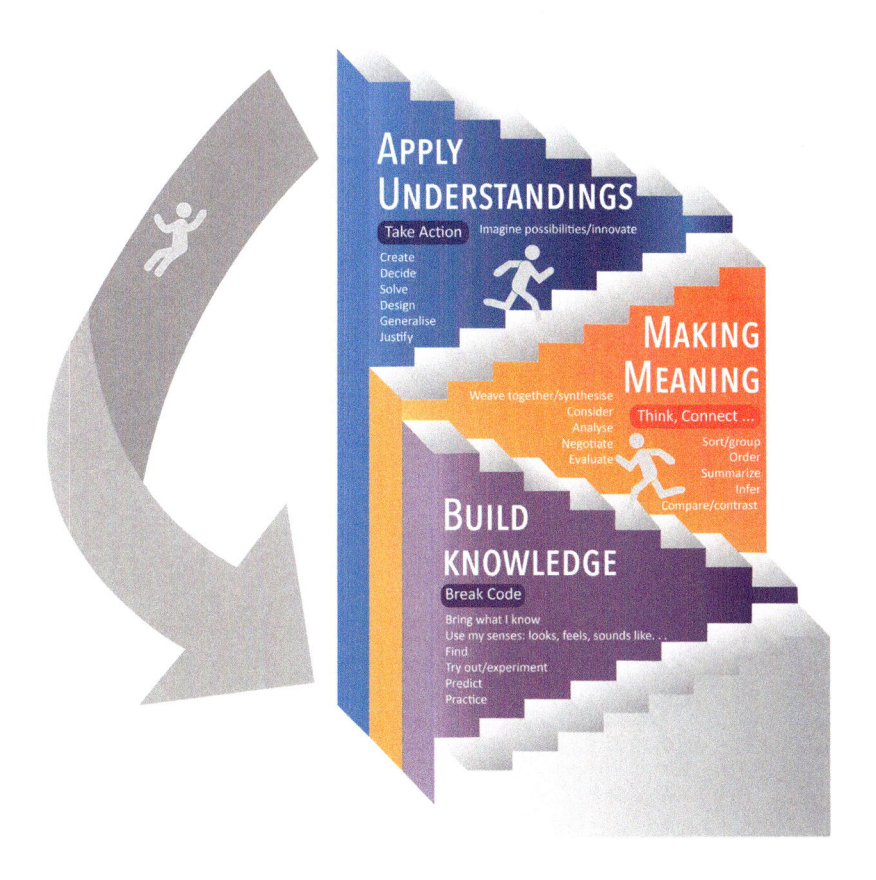

Planning your live lessons

When you start planning your life lessons, I encourage you to consider the content by looking at it through the eyes of the learner. What is most valuable and useful to them?

You can use the infographic above for inspiration when you plan **how to take the students through the phases of the learning process**. The agenda outline will help you plan your lessons. Make sure you help your students understand the milestone in the lesson by sharing what they need to KNOW and WHY and HOW to make sense of it. And finally, how they can APPLY the new knowledge to integrate what they are learning.

The agenda outline

An agenda outline for your live lessons can look like this:

Time Estimate	Agenda outline *Follows the structure in the storyboard*	Keywords *Key areas you want to cover*	Notes *What happened*
	Introduction – Learning Goal		
	Why		
	What		
	How		
	Apply		
	Q&A		
	Recap and what's next		

THE ULTIMATE COURSE CREATION GUIDE

The table below show you an example of how I have used the outline when planning one of the live lessons in my flagship course.

Time	Topic	Keywords	Notes
5	Introduction	Welcome Overall Learning Goal for YOU Create a course to SHARE Unique knowledge and generate revenue Question - answer in the chat: WHY? meaningful to the audience Recommend beta test Today 1st step: How To Easily Find Your Really Helpful Online Education Topic!	
10	Why	Why do we buy a course? Course transformation	
10	What	Point A -> Point B - GPS Why you? Your journey and uniqued combination as their guide 'Like Kind' How you build KLT	
10	How	Your unique combination -> guide in transformation The course transformation for your audience, their burning desire	
10	Apply	Fill out your unique course transformation worksheet Your Audience Burning Desire Worksheet	
5-10	Q&A	Questions from the audience	
5	Recap and what's next	Main points recap - what's your most important takeaway? Chat Next week: How To Write And Test Your Irresistible Online Course Offer	

Creating slides

If you choose to do talking-head style videos where you record yourself talking while showing slides there are some simple recommendations for creating slides:

- Simple visuals
- Only little text, keywords you read aloud
- Have each point show up as you speak

You can use Google slides, PowerPoint, Canva, etc.

To make it easier for yourself, you can create a rough outline first and then do a walk-through of the timing and the key content. And remember, you can always refine the slides afterward.

Practice

It is important to practice before each live session:

- Practice your presentation with slides and timing
- Test connection, camera, audio, and recording
- Remember, it doesn't have to be perfect

Running the live session

Make sure you are recording your session and upload the recording for replay.

Do your presentation and learn from the experience. Enjoy! You are presenting your unique knowledge to an audience who wants to hear what you have to say. And remember to ask for questions and feedback.

Questions for reflection

After the session, write some notes for yourself:

- What went well?
- What went not so well?
- What do I want to keep?
- What do I want to skip?
- What do I want to add?

Questions for reflection about the learning outcome and progress of your students:

- What did I want the students to learn?
- How did the different learning activities during the lesson help them get the desired outcome?
- How did I know that my students reached the goals of the lesson? If not, what could I do differently?

Improve Your Course for the Relaunch

After each lesson and course, set aside time to review your notes about the classes, student progress, and outcome. Did they reach the desired result? Did they get to Point B?

Spend some time on reflection and make the necessary adjustments for your next launch.

You can use the infographic below as an example of the cycle of continuous learning as you review the feedback you collected after each session and the outcomes your students achieved.

THE CYCLE OF CONTINUOUS LEARNING

1. MAKE AN INFORMED FIRST ATTEMPT

Execute the task to the best of your current ability

Use knowledge about past attempts or likely outcomes to make your first effort as effective as possible

2. REFLECT AND REDESIGN APPROACH

Consider outcomes/performance of attempt:
- What worked?
- What did not work and needs to change?
- Is there anything new you should try?

Redesign your approach, incorporating your learnings

3. MAKE AN IMPROVED ATTEMPT

Perform the task again, explicity focusing on incorporating your learnings from the last attempt

Emphasize what worked, leave out what failed, and add one or two new elements that your last attempt suggested might help

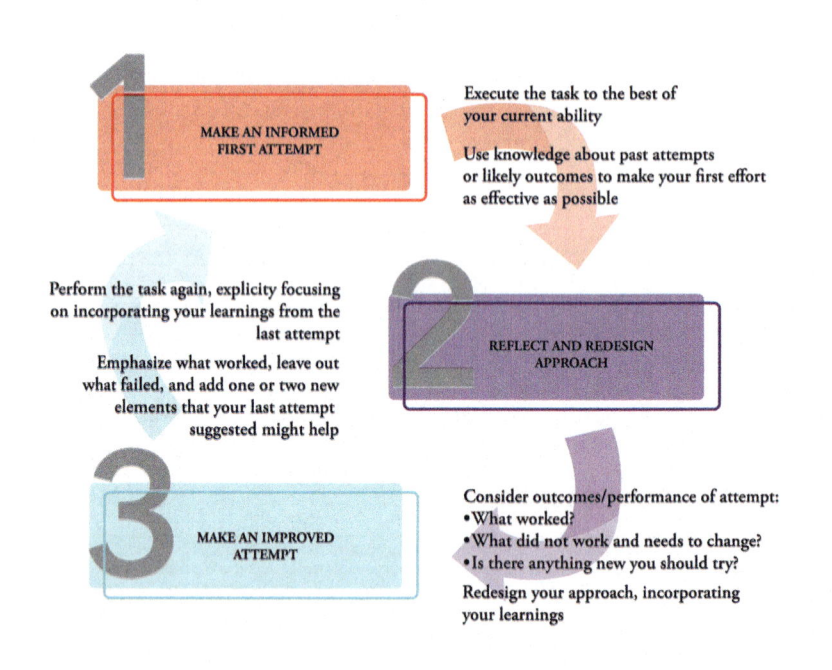

THE ULTIMATE COURSE CREATION GUIDE

Get testimonials

After the first test of your course, get testimonials you can use to strengthen your social proof on your sales page for the relaunch and your website.

In the text box below, you will find your lesson agenda outline. You can use this outline to plan each lesson both live and pre-recorded lessons.

Your Lesson Agenda Outline

Time Estimate	Agenda outline *Follows the structure in the storyboard*	Keywords *Key areas you want to cover*	Notes *What happened*
	Introduction – Learning Goal		✏️
	Why		✏️
	What		✏️
	How		✏️
	Apply		✏️
	Q&A		✏️
	Recap and what's next		✏️

Questions for reflection

After the session, write some notes for yourself:

- What went well?
- What went not so well?
- What do I want to keep?
- What do I want to skip?
- What do I want to add?

WEEK 8

> **Questions for reflection about the learning outcome and progress of your students:**
>
> - What did I want the students to learn?
> - How did the different learning activities during the lesson help them get the desired outcome?
> - How did I know that my students reached the goals of the lesson? If not, what could I do differently?

This basic lesson plan outline can be used for many purposes. You can use it when you plan a workshop, the content of your lessons in your online course, or the tasks in a workbook. You can also use the template to prepare your webinar's outline, as seen in the example below.

Lesson plan outline template for a webinar

Webinar title:

After the webinar, the students will be able to:

Know WHY, WHAT, HOW (basic idea), APPLY—WHO (Who they can go to for help)

In the webinar, they will learn:

- Key point 1:
- Key point 2:
- Key point 3:

Outline

Time	Topic	Notes
	Welcome	
	Introductions	
	Program	
	Why is this important?	
	What they need to know	
	How to implement (Basic idea)	
	How to apply/ get your help	
	Wrap up	

Use the outline to plan your webinar. Below you will find the other elements that go into planning a webinar sales funnel.

1. Create and Set Up Your Webinar
2. Create an Email Campaign
3. Set a Closing Strategy
4. Launch and Test
5. Evaluate and Repeat

WEEK 8

WEBINAR SALES FUNNEL
FOR YOUR COURSE RELAUNCH(ES)

1. Create and Set Up Your Webinar
Create an outline and slides to support your presentation.

2. Create an Email Campaign
Get people from your email list to your webinar with an Email Campaign.

3. Set a Closing Strategy
Where your customers go after the webinar. Link to your course sales page or book a call.

4. Launch and Test
Invite a segment of your email list to register for the webinar. Test and track results. Goal 3% conversion.

5. Evaluate and Repeat
Make an improved attempt based on your learnings from this launch.

Congratulations! If you have followed all the steps in this book, you now have a course ready for your first launch.

Take some time to celebrate this important step toward growing your business with an online course.

WHAT'S NEXT?

Remember creating a course is the beginning of an exciting journey of growing your business and helping more people in the process.

Having an online course is a great asset for you, your students, and your business. Remember that the course and other programs can be one of the many services you offer as you expand your business model and grow your business. Some people will want to get more specific and personalized help and guidance. As you expand your business model, you can create upsells with group and individual consulting and different levels of support from **YOU DO** to **WE DO** to **DONE FOR YOU**.

This means that your course is one of the components in your business model. As you grow your business, you want to lead people from your course to get more help through the other products and services you provide.

Like Dr. Ivan Misner emphasizes in his foreword, **networking** is one of the key strategies to get leads for your business and it is probably also one of the cheapest ways to convert leads to customers. I recommend you read *Networking Like a Pro, Second Edition* by Dr. Ivan Misner for inspiration. Here's the link:

https://www.amazon.com/Networking-Like-Pro-Contacts-Connections/dp/1599186047/

WHAT'S NEXT?

Another important strategy to grow your profitability is to **post content consistently** on social media to build your visibility or credibility as an industry expert. I have a course that teaches you how to write a copy that people will actually love to read.

https://courses.sophiehiggins.com/courses/how-to-write-great-copy-people-love-to-read

And remember to get the **FREE companion course** that comes as my gift to you with this book. Get access by following the link.

https://courses.sophiehiggins.com/courses/the-ultimate-course-creation-guide-how-to-grow-your-business-with-an-online-course?coupon=freewithultimatebook

If you want a **more in-depth explanation of how to take each step** you are welcome to join the course that follows and explains each of the steps of this book in detail. If you follow the link here in this book, you get 50 percent off the regular course price.

https://courses.sophiehiggins.com/courses/Create-Meaningful-Online-Courses-And-Grow-Passive-Income?coupon=ultimateguide

You can also book a **FREE 15-minute call** with me to learn more about how I can help you create your online course.

https://calendly.com/sophiehiggins/15

I'm here to help you **succeed** and build the business and the life you want with online courses as an integral part of your business.

https://sophiehiggins.com